LET'S EXPLORE THE JUNGLE

Have you ever thought of exploring the Jungle?

Find a wide range of interesting information that will help you understand and discover what a jungle is and why they are so unique and amazing.

A jungle is a land covered with dense trees, wild tangles of vegetation and dangerous animals. Jungle is the densest part of a rainforest.

Jungles only comprise around 6% of the planet's surface area, but more than 50% of all species live there.

The Amazon Jungle which contains 10% of the world's known species, is the largest jungle in the world.

Ample sunlight in a jungle creates dense areas of plants and vegetation that can be difficult to navigate.

It is estimated that 90 % of all jungle animals and plants live among its leaves.

Jungle is a mysterious place
filled with unique and exotic
animals. All of these animals
are captivating in their own
ways, however, some of them
should be left alone.

Here are some of the animals that live in the jungle.

The tiger is the largest cat species. Tigers can reach a length of up to 3.3 metres and weigh as much as 300 kilograms. tiger prefers denser vegetation, for which its camouflage colouring is ideally suited.

The ocelot is a wild cat distributed extensively within South America. Ocelots are carnivores, they eat animals such as rodents, rabbits, young deer, birds, snakes and fish.

A tapir is a large
herbivorous mammal.
Tapirs preferred
habitats are woodlands
and dense grassy
areas with a close
water source such as
lake or river.

The orangutans spend most of their time in trees. Most of the day is spent feeding, resting, and travelling. Orangutans are among the most intelligent primates.

Gibbons swing from branch to branch for distances of up to 15 m. They are the fastest and most agile of all tree-dwelling, nonflying mammals.

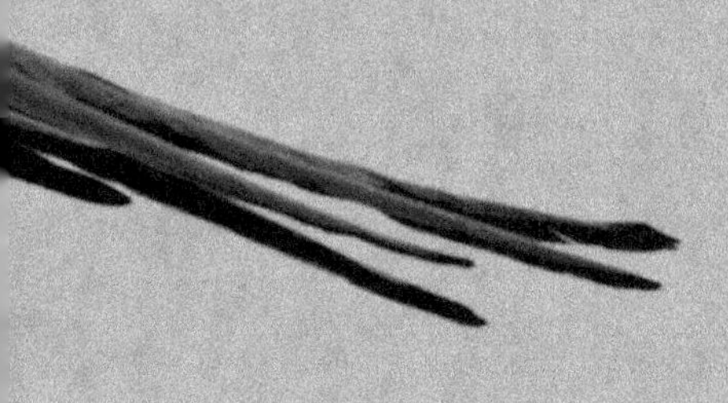

Hyacinth macaw is a parrot native to South America. The hyacinth macaw is the largest parrot by length in the world.

Poison dart frog are endemic to humid, tropical environments of Central and South America. They can be found in trees, under leaves and logs and rocks on the floor of the forest.

An anaconda is a
large snake found in
tropical South America.
Anacondas live near
rivers, lakes and
swamps. Anaconda
is nocturnal animal,
which means that it
hunts during the night.